AF379284

INTRODUCTION

"Whether you like or dislike the Bangtan Boys (BTS) are the very example that with determination, perseverance and discipline, you can achieve anything you set your mind to. All you need is the will to go all the way and believe in yourself. As an ARMY,
I'm immensely proud of my idols and, through their journey, I've learned that dreams are within reach for anyone who dares to pursue them.
This book is a heartfelt tribute to BTS and the profound impact they have had on my life and the lives of ARMYs everywhere. Within these pages you will find a collection of inspirational quotes, each reflecting the unique personality and wisdom of each BTS members.
So let's embark on this journey of self-discovery and empowerment, drawing strength from the words of these remarkable individuals who have touched our hearts and souls."

"What a relief, we are seven"
BTS

NAMJOON
INSPIRATIONS QUOTES

"True maturity lies
 in accepting
your flaws and
striving to improve them."

NAMJOON INSPIRATIONS QUOTES

"Maturity is understanding
that growth requires both
successes and failures."

NAMJOON INSPIRATIONS QUOTES

"Wisdom is not just
measured by age but
by the lessons
we learn along the way."

NAMJOON INSPIRATIONS QUOTES

"Maturity means
taking responsibility
for your actions
and their consequences."

NAMJOON INSPIRATIONS QUOTES

"Embrace change,
 for it is the catalyst for
personal growth and maturity."

NAMJOON INSPIRATIONS QUOTES

"Maturity is realizing
that patience is a
 virtue that leads
to greater rewards."

NAMJOON INSPIRATIONS QUOTES

"Self-reflection is
the path to self-awareness
and emotional maturity."

NAMJOON INSPIRATIONS QUOTES

"Maturity is knowing
when to speak up
and when to listen."

NAMJOON INSPIRATIONS QUOTES

"True maturity is
being kind even
 in the face of adversity."

NAMJOON INSPIRATIONS QUOTES

"Maturity is understanding
that everyone's journey is
 unique and deserving of respect."

NAMJOON INSPIRATIONS QUOTES

"Maturity is learning
from your mistakes
and striving to do better."

NAMJOON INSPIRATIONS QUOTES

"Strength lies in
 emotional maturity,
where you can face
 your vulnerabilities head-on."

NAMJOON INSPIRATIONS QUOTES

"Maturity is being
open-minded and
willing to learn from others."

NAMJOON INSPIRATIONS QUOTES

"True maturity is
found in humility,
not in arrogance."

NAMJOON INSPIRATIONS QUOTES

"Maturity is treating others with empathy and compassion."

NAMJOON INSPIRATIONS QUOTES

"Wisdom comes
with maturity,
as you gain
a broader perspective on life."

NAMJOON INSPIRATIONS QUOTES

"Maturity is understanding
that forgiveness
is essential for personal growth."

NAMJOON INSPIRATIONS QUOTES

"True maturity is
being honest with yourself
 and others,
even when it's difficult."

NAMJOON INSPIRATIONS QUOTES

"Maturity is knowing
when to let go
 and when to hold on."

NAMJOON INSPIRATIONS QUOTES

"Self-confidence is
the mark of maturity,
as you believe in
your own abilities."

NAMJOON INSPIRATIONS QUOTES

"Maturity is recognizing
the value of hard work
 and perseverance."

NAMJOON INSPIRATIONS QUOTES

"Maturity means
being accountable
 for your choices
and their consequences."

NAMJOON INSPIRATIONS QUOTES

"True maturity is
 being aware of the impact
of your words
and actions on others."

"Maturity is accepting
that not everything
in life can be controlled."

NAMJOON INSPIRATIONS QUOTES

"Wisdom comes with maturity,
as you learn
to trust your intuition."

NAMJOON INSPIRATIONS QUOTES

"Maturity is finding
balance in all
aspects of your life."

NAMJOON INSPIRATIONS QUOTES

"Maturity is respecting
 boundaries and
understanding
the importance of consent."

NAMJOON INSPIRATIONS QUOTES

"True maturity is
acknowledging your weaknesses
and working
towards self-improvement."

NAMJOON INSPIRATIONS QUOTES

"Maturity is having
the courage to face
 your fears and overcome them."

NAMJOON INSPIRATIONS QUOTES

"Maturity means
 recognizing
the value of lifelong learning."

NAMJOON INSPIRATIONS QUOTES

"Maturity is being able
to forgive yourself and
let go of past mistakes."

NAMJOON INSPIRATIONS QUOTES

"True maturity is finding
peace within yourself
and radiating it to others."

NAMJOON INSPIRATIONS QUOTES

"Maturity is understanding
that success is a journey,
not a destination."

NAMJOON INSPIRATIONS QUOTES

"Maturity means taking
care of your physical
and mental well-being."

NAMJOON INSPIRATIONS QUOTES

"Maturity is accepting
that not everyone
will understand
or agree with you, and that's okay."

NAMJOON INSPIRATIONS QUOTES

"True maturity
 is being able to handle criticism
gracefully and learn from it."

NAMJOON INSPIRATIONS QUOTES

"Maturity is realizing
that true happiness comes
 from within,
not from external validation."

NAMJOON INSPIRATIONS QUOTES

"Maturity means
having the courage
to stand up for
what you believe in."

NAMJOON INSPIRATIONS QUOTES

"Maturity is being
accountable for
your mistakes and
making amends."

NAMJOON INSPIRATIONS QUOTES

"True maturity is being able
to see beyond yourself and
contribute to the greater good."

NAMJOON INSPIRATIONS QUOTES

"Maturity is recognizing
 that change is constant
and adapting accordingly."

NAMJOON INSPIRATIONS QUOTES

"Maturity means
valuing relationships
and investing time
and effort into nurturing them."

NAMJOON INSPIRATIONS QUOTES

"Maturity is
 knowing when to prioritize
your own well-being
and set boundaries."

NAMJOON INSPIRATIONS QUOTES

"True maturity is
having a strong sense of self-worth
that is not dependent on others' opinions."

NAMJOON INSPIRATIONS QUOTES

"Maturity is
treating everyone with kindness
and respect,
regardless of their background."

ans

to handle success
with grace and humility."

NAMJOON INSPIRATIONS QUOTES

"Maturity is
 being able to appreciate
the beauty in simplicity."

NAMJOON INSPIRATIONS QUOTES

"True maturity is
understanding that true strength
lies in vulnerability."

NAMJOON INSPIRATIONS QUOTES

"Maturity is
being open to different perspectives
 and willing to learn from them."

NAMJOON INSPIRATIONS QUOTES

"Maturity means
 living authentically and staying
true to yourself, no matter what."

SEOKJIN
INSPIRATIONS QUOTES

SEOKJIN INSPIRATIONS QUOTES

"Confidence is
believing in yourself
even when others doubt you."

SEOKJIN INSPIRATIONS QUOTES

"True confidence
 comes from embracing
your strengths and weaknesses."

SEOKJIN INSPIRATIONS QUOTES

"Your uniqueness
is your greatest asset;
 let it shine with confidence."

SEOKJIN INSPIRATIONS QUOTES

"Confidence is
not about being perfect;
it's about being comfortable
 with who you are."

SEOKJIN INSPIRATIONS QUOTES

"Believe in your abilities,
for you are capable
of achieving great things."

SEOKJIN INSPIRATIONS QUOTES

"Confidence is
having faith in your journey,
even when the path seems uncertain."

SEOKJIN INSPIRATIONS QUOTES

"Embrace self-love and
watch your confidence
soar to new heights."

"True confidence
is rooted in self-acceptance
and self-worth."

SEOKJIN INSPIRATIONS QUOTES

"Be fearless
in the pursuit of your dreams;
confidence will guide you."

SEOKJIN INSPIRATIONS QUOTES

"Confidence is
knowing that you are
 deserving of love and respect."

SEOKJIN INSPIRATIONS QUOTES

"Your voice matters;
speak up with confidence
and make a difference."

SEOKJIN INSPIRATIONS QUOTES

"Confidence is
 walking into a room
with your head held high,
owning your presence."

SEOKJIN INSPIRATIONS QUOTES

"Believe in
 your ideas and abilities,
for confidence
 is the fuel of innovation."

SEOKJIN INSPIRATIONS QUOTES

"True confidence is
being unapologetically yourself,
without seeking validation."

SEOKJIN INSPIRATIONS QUOTES

"Confidence is
the belief that you are capable
of overcoming any challenge."

SEOKJIN INSPIRATIONS QUOTES

"Embrace your flaws,
 for they are what make
you beautifully unique."

SEOKJIN INSPIRATIONS QUOTES

"Confidence is
not about being better than others;
it's about being
the best version of yourself."

SEOKJIN INSPIRATIONS QUOTES

"Believe in your worthiness
and watch your confidence
radiate to those around you."

SEOKJIN INSPIRATIONS QUOTES

"True confidence is
 not boastful;
it's quietly assured."

SEOKJIN INSPIRATIONS QUOTES

"Confidence is
 stepping out of your comfort zone
and embracing new experiences."

SEOKJIN INSPIRATIONS QUOTES

"Embrace your talents with confidence,
knowing that they
 have the power to inspire others."

SEOKJIN INSPIRATIONS QUOTES

"Confidence is
not based on external validation;
it comes from within."

SEOKJIN INSPIRATIONS QUOTES

"Believe in your potential,
for confidence
is the key to unlocking it."

SEOKJIN INSPIRATIONS QUOTES

"True confidence is rooted in resilience, bouncing back stronger after every setback."

SEOKJIN INSPIRATIONS QUOTES

"Confidence
is trusting your instincts
and making decisions with conviction."

SEOKJIN INSPIRATIONS QUOTES

"Embrace
 your individuality and
let your confidence
 be a beacon of inspiration."

SEOKJIN INSPIRATIONS QUOTES

"Confidence is
not about being loud;
it's about speaking with conviction."

SEOKJIN INSPIRATIONS QUOTES

"Believe in
your worthiness of love
and success,
for confidence attracts abundance."

SEOKJIN INSPIRATIONS QUOTES

"True confidence is
not arrogant; it's humble
 and appreciative of others' strengths."

SEOKJIN INSPIRATIONS QUOTES

"Confidence is
embracing challenges as opportunities
for growth and self-improvement."

"Embrace your body
with confidence,
for it's a vessel
 that carries your beautiful soul."

SEOKJIN INSPIRATIONS QUOTES

"Confidence is
knowing that you are enough,
just as you are."

SEOKJIN INSPIRATIONS QUOTES

"Believe in your dreams,
for confidence is the bridge that
turns them into reality."

"True confidence is
contagious; it inspires others
to believe in themselves."

Inspire

SEOKJIN INSPIRATIONS QUOTES

"Confidence is
not about fitting in; it's about
standing out with authenticity."

SEOKJIN INSPIRATIONS QUOTES

"Embrace
your uniqueness with confidence,
for it sets you apart in a crowded world."

SEOKJIN INSPIRATIONS QUOTES

"Confidence is
knowing that your worth is
 not defined by others' opinions."

SEOKJIN INSPIRATIONS QUOTES

"Believe in
your strengths, for confidence
is the magnet that attracts success."

SEOKJIN INSPIRATIONS QUOTES

"True confidence is
not afraid of failure; it sees it
as a stepping stone to growth."

SEOKJIN INSPIRATIONS QUOTES

"Confidence is
 being comfortable in your own skin,
without seeking validation from others."

SEOKJIN INSPIRATIONS QUOTES

"Embrace
your passions with confidence,
for they fuel your purpose."

SEOKJIN INSPIRATIONS QUOTES

"Confidence is
not about being the best;
it's about being your best."

SEOKJIN INSPIRATIONS QUOTES

"Believe in
your ability to make a difference,
for confidence empowers change."

SEOKJIN INSPIRATIONS QUOTES

"True confidence is
not about superiority;
it's about lifting others up
 with kindness."

SEOKJIN INSPIRATIONS QUOTES

"Confidence is
standing up for what you believe in,
even in the face of opposition."

SEOKJIN INSPIRATIONS QUOTES

"Embrace
your accomplishments with confidence,
for they are a testament to your growth."

SEOKJIN INSPIRATIONS QUOTES

"Confidence is
not about perfection;
it's about embracing your journey,
flaws and all."

SEOKJIN INSPIRATIONS QUOTES

"Believe in
your worthiness of happiness,
 for confidence opens the door to joy."

SEOKJIN INSPIRATIONS QUOTES

"True confidence is
not arrogant;
it's secure in its own skin."

SEOKJIN INSPIRATIONS QUOTES

"Confidence is
believing in yourself, even
when the world tries to bring you down."

YOONGI
INSPIRATIONS QUOTES

"Hard work is the foundation
upon which your dreams are built;
it paves the way to success."

YOONGI INSPIRATIONS QUOTES

"Courage is
the fire within that fuels
your relentless pursuit of your dreams."

"Be brave
enough to defy the odds
and work tirelessly to achieve
 what others think is impossible."

YOONGI INSPIRATIONS QUOTES

"Courage is
not the absence of fear,
but the audacity to face your fears
 head-on and conquer them."

"Success comes
to those who dare to dream
and are willing to put in the effort
to make those dreams a reality."

YOONGI INSPIRATIONS QUOTES

"Hard work
is the key that unlocks the door
to your aspirations; without it,
 success remains a distant dream."

YOONGI INSPIRATIONS QUOTES

"Be fearless
 in the pursuit of your goals,
for your courage
 and hard work will break down
any barriers in your way."

"Courage is
the strength to persist
when faced with challenges, setbacks,
and moments of doubt."

"Hard work is
the secret ingredient that turns ordinary
talent into extraordinary achievements."

"Be brave
enough to take risks, embrace failure,
and learn from it as you
continue to work towards your goals."

YOONGI INSPIRATIONS QUOTES

"Courage is
having the determination
to keep going even when
you feel exhausted and overwhelmed."

YOONGI INSPIRATIONS QUOTES

"Success is
not handed to you;
it is earned through countless
 sleepless nights and
unyielding perseverance."

"Be relentless in your
pursuit of greatness; let your
hard work speak volumes about
your dedication and commitment."

"Courage is being
unapologetically true to yourself and
pursuing your passion wholeheartedly."

YOONGI INSPIRATIONS QUOTES

"Hard work is
the bridge between your dreams
 and their realization; it is the path
to transformation and growth."

YOONGI INSPIRATIONS QUOTES

"Be brave
enough to stand out,
to challenge the norm,
and to pave your own path
with your hard work and dedication."

"Courage is
the willingness to face criticism
and rejection, knowing that
they are mere stepping stones
on the journey to success."

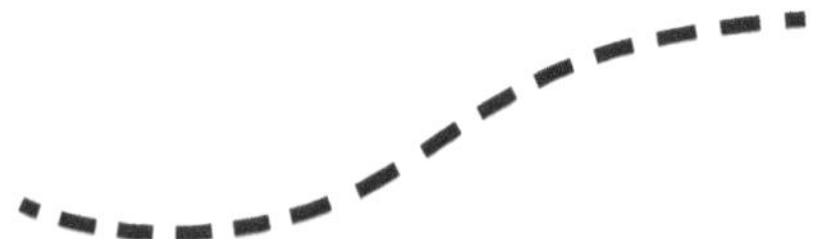

YOONGI INSPIRATIONS QUOTES

"Success belongs
to those who have the courage
 to dream big and the work ethic
to turn those dreams into tangible
achievements."

"Be unwavering in
your commitment to your craft,
for hard work is the key that unlocks
the door to mastery."

"Courage is pushing
yourself beyond your limits,
constantly striving for improvement,
and refusing to settle for mediocrity."

YOONGI INSPIRATIONS QUOTES

"Hard work is
 the investment you make in yourself,
knowing that the dividends
will be worth every ounce of effort."

YOONGI INSPIRATIONS QUOTES

"Be bold
enough to challenge yourself,
to step out of your comfort zone,
and to push the boundaries
of your potential through hard work."

"Courage is
the voice that whispers, 'You can do it,'
even when doubt
tries to drown out your dreams."

I can do this

YOONGI INSPIRATIONS QUOTES

"Success is
not a destination;
it is a journey fueled by your unwavering
courage and tireless hard work."

YOONGI INSPIRATIONS QUOTES

"Be persistent
in your pursuit of excellence,
 for hard work and determination are
the keys that open doors to endless
possibilities."

YOONGI INSPIRATIONS QUOTES

"Courage is having faith
in your abilities, even
when the world tries to
shake your confidence."

YOONGI INSPIRATIONS QUOTES

"Hard work is the sweat, tears,
and sacrifices that lay the
groundwork for your achievements."

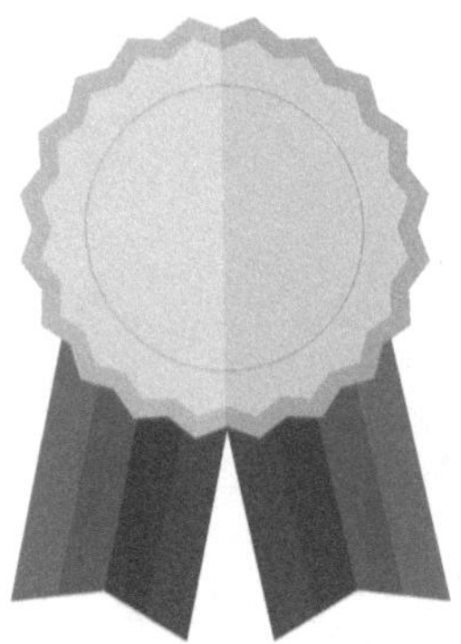

"Be fearless in the face of adversity, knowing that your courage and hard work will propel you forward, no matter the challenges."

"Courage is standing up
for what you believe in, staying
true to yourself, and working
towards your vision,
despite the obstacles."

"Success requires both
courage and hard work;
they are the twin forces that
propel you towards your goals."

YOONGI INSPIRATIONS QUOTES

"Be brave enough to pursue your passions, invest in your growth, and trust in the process of hard work and dedication."

YOONGI INSPIRATIONS QUOTES

"Courage is the strength to
keep going when everything
seems to be falling apart, holding
onto your dreams with unwavering
determination."

YOONGI INSPIRATIONS QUOTES

"Hard work is the anthem
of the dedicated; it is the rhythm
that drives you closer
to the symphony of your dreams."

YOONGI INSPIRATIONS QUOTES

"Be bold
enough to dream big, work hard,
and make your mark on the world
through your unwavering courage
 and relentless efforts."

"Courage is the
unwavering belief in yourself,
even when the odds seem
 insurmountable."

YOONGI INSPIRATIONS QUOTES

"Success is
the culmination of countless
hours of hard work, discipline,
and the bravery to never
give up on your dreams."

"Be resilient in the
face of failure, using it as
a stepping stone to grow,
learn, and become stronger
through your hard work."

"Courage is the light
that guides you through the
darkest moments, reminding
you of your strength and potential."

YOONGI INSPIRATIONS QUOTES

"Hard work is the secret
ingredient that transforms
dreams into reality, turning
aspirations into tangible achievements."

"Be courageous enough
to embrace uncertainty,
for it is in those moments that
your true capabilities shine
through your hard work."

"Courage is the fuel that
propels you forward
 when doubt tries to hold you back;
it is the fire within that ignites your
determination."

YOONGI INSPIRATIONS QUOTES

"Success is not for
the faint-hearted; it is the result
of unwavering courage
and the unwavering dedication
to your craft."

"Be bold enough to pursue
your dreams without hesitation,
knowing that your hard work
will carry you closer to their realization."

YOONGI INSPIRATIONS QUOTES

"Courage is taking the first step,
even when the path ahead is
 unknown, trusting in your ability
to navigate through hard work."

YOONGI INSPIRATIONS QUOTES

"Hard work is he language
of champions, spoken by those
who are committed
to pushing their limits
and achieving greatness."

"Be fearless in embracing failure,
for it is through your hard
work and perseverance
that failure becomes a stepping
stone towards success."

"Courage is not the absence
of doubt; it is the choice to keep going
in spite of it, fueled by your
unwavering work ethic."

YOONGI INSPIRATIONS QUOTES

"Success comes to those
who have the courage to dream,
the resilience to work hard,
and the audacity to turn those
dreams into reality."

"Be relentless in
your pursuit of your goals,
knowing that your courage
and hard work will set you apart
 and propel you towards success."

"Courage is the belief that you
are capable of achieving
greatness and the commitment to work
tirelessly towards making it a reality."

HOSEOK
INSPIRATIONS QUOTES

HOSEOK INSPIRATIONS QUOTES

"Embrace each day
with a smile, for positivity is
the fuel that ignites our dreams."

"Spread your wings
and let your positivity soar
higher than the sky."

HOSEOK INSPIRATIONS QUOTES

"Dance to the rhythm
of positivity and watch
how it transforms your world."

HOSEOK INSPIRATIONS QUOTES

"In every challenge, find an opportunity to shine and let your positivity guide you through."

HOSEOK INSPIRATIONS QUOTES

"Let your laughter
be contagious and
your positivity be infectious."

HOSEOK INSPIRATIONS QUOTES

"Just like sunshine,
your positivity has the power
to brighten even the darkest days."

HOSEOK INSPIRATIONS QUOTES

"Believe in
yourself and your dreams,
and let your positive energy
light the way."

HOSEOK INSPIRATIONS QUOTES

"With a positive mindset
,every setback becomes a stepping stone
towards success."

HOSEOK INSPIRATIONS QUOTES

"Surround yourself
with positive vibes,
and watch how it elevates your spirit."

HOSEOK INSPIRATIONS QUOTES

"Let your positivity
radiate like a beacon of hope,
inspiring others along the way."

"Find joy in the little things,
 and let your positive attitude amplify
the happiness in your life."

HOSEOK INSPIRATIONS QUOTES

"When you have a positive mindset,
the world becomes a brighter place."

HOSEOK INSPIRATIONS QUOTES

"When life throws lemons at you, be the one who turns them into a refreshing glass of positivity."

HOSEOK INSPIRATIONS QUOTES

"Choose to dance
in the rain of positivity rather than
waiting for the storm to pass."

HOSEOK INSPIRATIONS QUOTES

"Your smile has the
power to brighten the world,
so wear it proudly and spread positivity."

"Even in the face of adversity,
be the source of light and positivity that
never wavers."

HOSEOK INSPIRATIONS QUOTES

"Let your positive energy
 flow through your actions and create
a ripple effect of happiness."

"The power of positivity
lies within you. Harness it and watch
miracles unfold."

HOSEOK INSPIRATIONS QUOTES

"Be the ray of sunshine
that breaks through the clouds,
illuminating the world with positivity."

"Never underestimate
the impact of your positive words.
They have the power to uplift souls."

I deserve good things

HOSEOK INSPIRATIONS QUOTES

"In a world full of negativity,
be the refreshing breeze of positivity that
brings joy to others."

"Your positive attitude is
the compass that guides you towards
a life filled with abundance."

HOSEOK INSPIRATIONS QUOTES

"When you radiate positivity,
you attract endless possibilities and
blessings."

"Let your positive energy
shine so brightly that it inspires others to
embrace their own light."

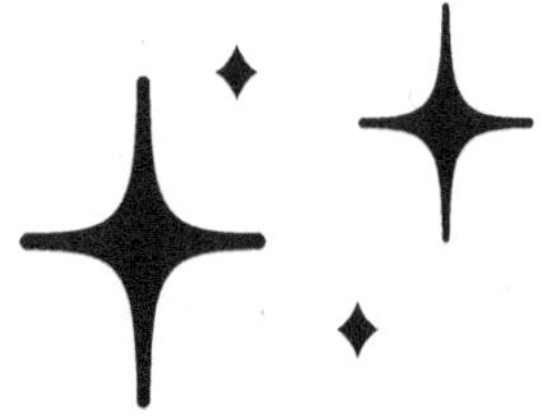

HOSEOK INSPIRATIONS QUOTES

"Stay true to your positive nature,
 even when faced with doubts. Your belief
can move mountains."

HOSEOK INSPIRATIONS QUOTES

"When you dance with positivity,
 the whole universe moves in harmony
with your dreams."

HOSEOK INSPIRATIONS QUOTES

"Your unwavering
belief in yourself is the fuel
that propels you towards greatness.
Stay positive."

"Leave a trail of positivity
wherever you go, and
watch how it transforms lives."

HOSEOK INSPIRATIONS QUOTES

"Embrace the power of optimism,
for it has the ability to turn dreams into
reality."

HOSEOK INSPIRATIONS QUOTES

"See the beauty in every moment,
 and let your positive outlook paint your
world with vibrant colors."

HOSEOK INSPIRATIONS QUOTES

"You have within you the power
 to create a positive change.
Believe in yourself and make it happen."

"In the dance of life, let
 your positive energy be the
rhythm that keeps you moving forward."

HOSEOK INSPIRATIONS QUOTES

"Choose positivity
as your daily mantra
, and watch how it shapes your destiny."

HOSEOK INSPIRATIONS QUOTES

"Even in the midst of challenges,
your positive mindset can turn stumbling
blocks into stepping stones."

HOSEOK INSPIRATIONS QUOTES

"Fill your heart
with gratitude and
your mind with positivity,
and watch how your world transforms."

"The key to happiness
lies in embracing positivity
and letting it guide you on your journey."

HOSEOK INSPIRATIONS QUOTES

"Choose optimism over pessimism,
 and unlock the door to a life filled with
endless possibilities."

HOSEOK INSPIRATIONS QUOTES

"Your positive spirit is contagious.
Spread it like wildfire and ignite the world
with hope."

HOSEOK INSPIRATIONS QUOTES

"Believe in the power
 of your dreams and let
your positive energy fuel your
pursuit of success."

HOSEOK INSPIRATIONS QUOTES

"Shine brightly like the sun,
for your positivity has the power
to light up the world."

HOSEOK INSPIRATIONS QUOTES

"Embrace your inner
sunshine and let it radiate joy
and warmth to those around you."

HOSEOK INSPIRATIONS QUOTES

"Just as the sun brings
 light to the world, let your vibrant spirit
bring light to every situation."

HOSEOK INSPIRATIONS QUOTES

"Be a beacon of positivity,
illuminating even the darkest corners
with your infectious smile."

"Like the sun,
let your energy
and passion rise each day,
 inspiring others to embrace
their own light."

HOSEOK INSPIRATIONS QUOTES

"Your presence is
 like a ray of sunshine,
bringing a sense of warmth
and happiness wherever you go."

"The world needs
your sunshine.
Embrace your uniqueness
 and let it shine brightly for all to see."

HOSEOK INSPIRATIONS QUOTES

"Don't be afraid
 to unleash your inner sun.
Embrace your authenticity
and let it light up the sky."

"Just as the sun rises each day,
rise with a positive attitude and a
determination to make a difference."

HOSEOK INSPIRATIONS QUOTES

"In a world filled with clouds,
be the sun that breaks through,
spreading rays of hope and positivity."

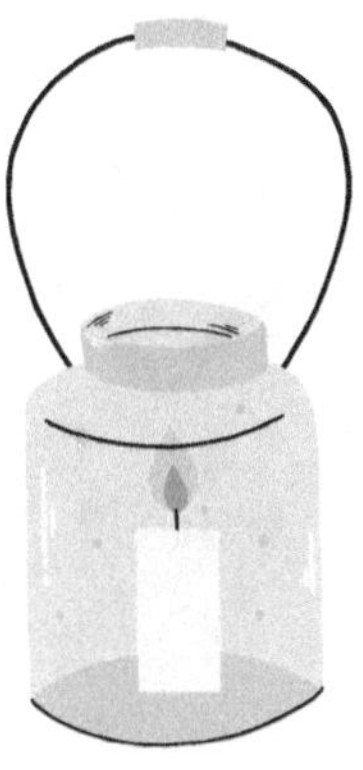

HOSEOK INSPIRATIONS QUOTES

"You have the power
to make a positive difference in the world.
Embrace it and let your light shine."

JIMIN
INSPIRATIONS QUOTES

"Love is
the greatest gift
we can give to our loved ones;
cherish them with all your heart."

JIMIN INSPIRATIONS QUOTES

"Appreciate the people
who bring joy to your life,
for they are the ones who
make it worth living."

"Love is
not just a feeling;
it is a verb that requires action
 and genuine care for your loved ones."

JIMIN INSPIRATIONS QUOTES

"Appreciate
the little moments
with your loved ones,
 for they are the ones
 that create beautiful memories."

"Love unconditionally,
for it is through love that
we find true happiness and fulfillment."

JIMIN INSPIRATIONS QUOTES

"Appreciate the uniqueness
of each person in your life;
they bring diversity
and beauty to your world."

JIMIN INSPIRATIONS QUOTES

"Love is
a language that needs
no words; it is felt through the actions
and kindness we show to our loved ones."

JIMIN INSPIRATIONS QUOTES

"Appreciate the support
 and encouragement
of your loved ones;
they are your pillars of strength."

"Love is not about possession;
it is about nurturing
and allowing your loved
ones to grow and flourish."

JIMIN INSPIRATIONS QUOTES

"Appreciate the laughter
and smiles shared
with your loved ones;
they are the music of your soul."

JIMIN INSPIRATIONS QUOTES

"Love is the bridge that connects hearts and souls, forging deep and meaningful connections with your loved ones."

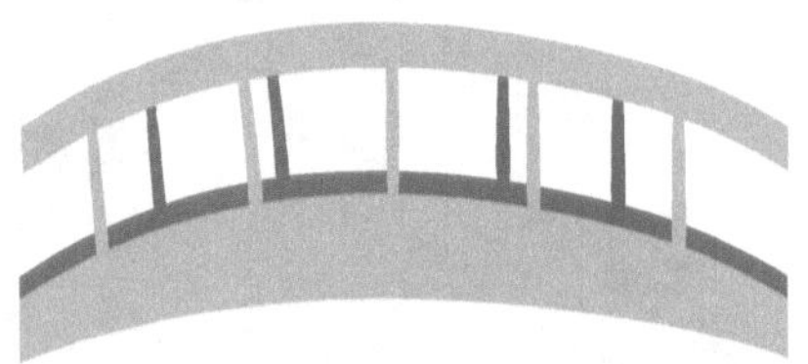

JIMIN INSPIRATIONS QUOTES

"Appreciate the lessons
learned from your loved ones;
they help shape you into the person
you are today."

"Love is
a continuous journey
of understanding, acceptance,
and forgiveness
towards your loved ones."

JIMIN INSPIRATIONS QUOTES

"Appreciate the presence
of your loved ones in your life,
for they bring warmth and light to
your darkest days."

"Love is
expressed through small
acts of kindness and gestures of affection
towards your loved ones."

JIMIN INSPIRATIONS QUOTES

"Appreciate
the sacrifices made by
your loved ones; their selflessness
is a testament to their love for you."

JIMIN INSPIRATIONS QUOTES

"Love is the foundation
that builds strong bonds and
creates a sense of belonging
among your loved ones."

JIMIN INSPIRATIONS QUOTES

"Appreciate
the comfort and solace
provided by your loved ones
during times of sadness and despair."

"Love is patient,
understanding, and
supportive of the growth
and dreams of your loved ones."

JIMIN INSPIRATIONS QUOTES

"Appreciate
the unique qualities
and talents of your loved ones; they
contribute to the richness of your life."

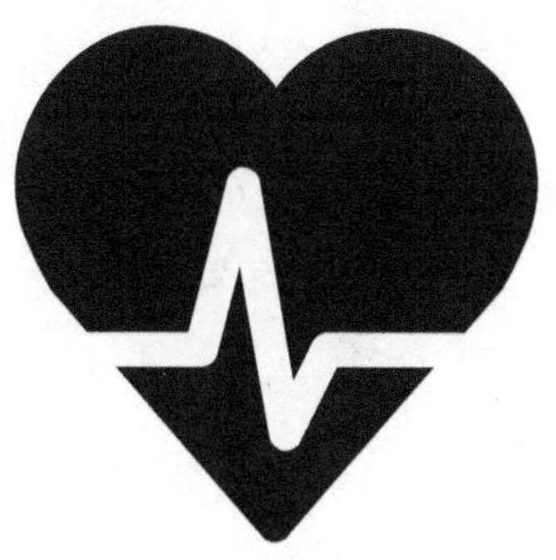

"Love is a beacon of hope
and encouragement,
inspiring your loved ones
to reach for their dreams."

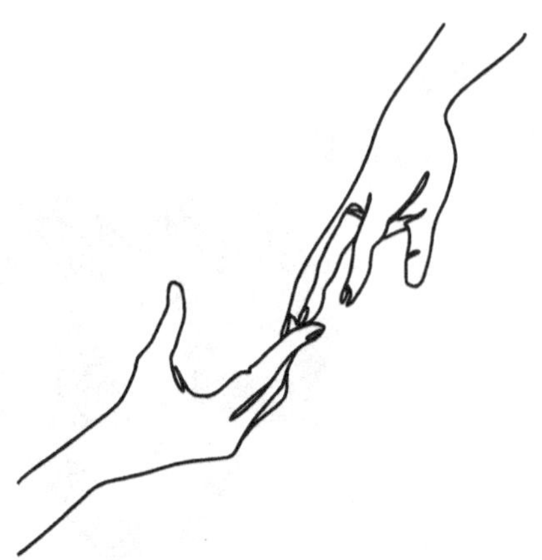

JIMIN INSPIRATIONS QUOTES

"Appreciate
the trust and vulnerability
shared with your loved ones;
it strengthens the bond between you."

"Love is a beautiful
 dance of care, respect, and
compassion with your loved ones."

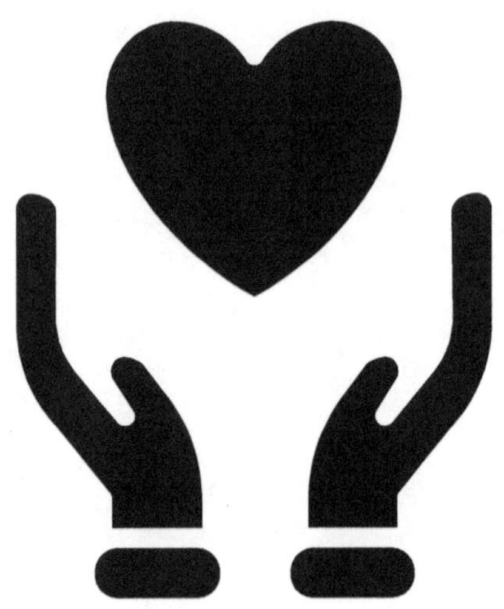

JIMIN INSPIRATIONS QUOTES

"Appreciate
the love and acceptance
of your loved ones,
for they see the beauty within you."

JIMIN INSPIRATIONS QUOTES

"Love is the greatest
source of strength; it
empowers you and your loved ones
to overcome any challenge."

JIMIN INSPIRATIONS QUOTES

"Appreciate
the unconditional love
and unwavering support
that your loved ones offer you."

"Love is not limited by distance;
it transcends physical boundaries
and connects hearts across the world."

JIMIN INSPIRATIONS QUOTES

"Appreciate
the wisdom and guidance
shared by your loved ones;
their experiences are
invaluable treasures."

"Love is
a gentle touch,
a warm embrace,
and a reassuring presence
for your loved ones."

JIMIN INSPIRATIONS QUOTES

"Appreciate the laughter
and joy shared with your
loved ones; they are
the sparks that light up your life."

"Love is the foundation of
a strong family, built on trust, respect,
and unwavering support for one another."

JIMIN INSPIRATIONS QUOTES

"Appreciate
the uniqueness of each relationship
with your loved ones;
they bring diverse colors
to your life's canvas."

"Love is
not about perfection;
it is about accepting and
embracing the imperfections
of your loved ones."

JIMIN INSPIRATIONS QUOTES

"Appreciate the growth
and transformation shared
 with your loved ones; they inspire you to
become a better version of yourself."

JIMIN INSPIRATIONS QUOTES

"Love is
the thread that weaves
the tapestry of beautiful memories
 with your loved ones."

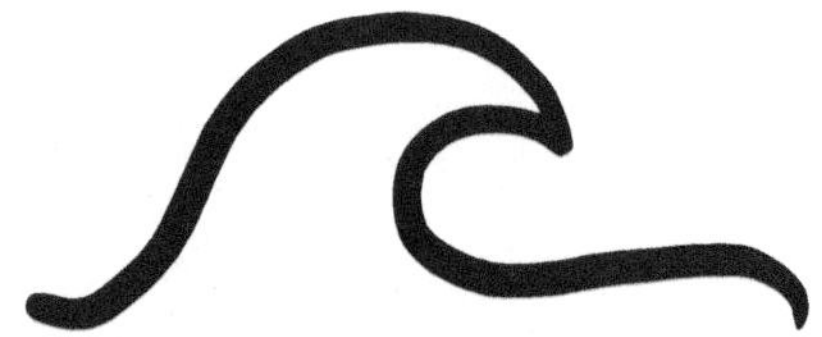

JIMIN INSPIRATIONS QUOTES

"Appreciate the kindness
 and compassion shown by
your loved ones; it is a reflection
of their deep love for you."

"Love is
a shield that protects
and nurtures your loved ones,
creating a safe space for them to be
themselves."

"Appreciate
the support and
encouragement of your loved ones;
they believe in
your dreams and cheer you on."

"Love is the melody
that harmonizes hearts, bringing joy and
serenity to your loved ones."

JIMIN INSPIRATIONS QUOTES

"Appreciate
the lessons of resilience
and strength learned from
your loved ones; they inspire you
to overcome any adversity."

"Love is a language spoken through acts of service, affection, and understanding towards your loved ones."

JIMIN INSPIRATIONS QUOTES

"Appreciate the love and care expressed
by your loved ones; they are
your guiding stars in the journey of life."

"Love is
a balm that heals wounds, so
othes pain, and brings comfort
to your loved ones."

JIMIN INSPIRATIONS QUOTES

"Appreciate
the shared dreams and
aspirations with your loved ones;
they become your biggest supporters
and collaborators."

JIMIN INSPIRATIONS QUOTES

"Love is the foundation of trust and loyalty, creating unbreakable bonds with your loved ones."

JIMIN INSPIRATIONS QUOTES

"Appreciate the resilience and
determination of your loved ones;
they inspire you
to never give up on your dreams."

JIMIN INSPIRATIONS QUOTES

"Love is
 a symphony of understanding,
empathy, and acceptance in your
relationships with your loved ones."

JIMIN INSPIRATIONS QUOTES

"Appreciate
the unconditional love and
acceptance provided by your loved ones;
it gives you the freedom
to be your authentic self."

JIMIN INSPIRATIONS QUOTES

"Love is the light that guides
and uplifts your loved ones,
illuminating their path
with warmth and hope."

JIMIN INSPIRATIONS QUOTES

"Appreciate the moments
of vulnerability and authenticity
 shared with your loved ones;
they strengthen the connection and
deepen the love between you."

TAEHYUNG
INSPIRATIONS QUOTES

TAEHYUNG INSPIRATIONS QUOTES

"Embrace who you are,
for there is beauty
in your uniqueness."

TAEHYUNG INSPIRATIONS QUOTES

"You are enough
just as you are.
Embrace your true self and shine."

TAEHYUNG INSPIRATIONS QUOTES

"Being yourself is
the most powerful and
liberating gift you can give to yourself."

"You don't need
to be someone else to be extraordinary.
Embrace your own greatness."

"The world needs your authentic self.
Don't be afraid to show
who you truly are."

"Your quirks
and imperfections are
what make you beautifully
and uniquely you."

TAEHYUNG INSPIRATIONS QUOTES

"Being okay
with being yourself is
the key to genuine happiness
and self-acceptance."

TAEHYUNG INSPIRATIONS QUOTES

"You are a masterpiece
in your own right.
Embrace your individuality
and let it shine."

TAEHYUNG INSPIRATIONS QUOTES

"You are not defined by others' opinions.
Be true to yourself and let
your light guide you."

"In a world that constantly tries to mold you, dare to be unapologetically yourself."

"Your authenticity is
 your superpower. Embrace it
and let it guide you on your journey."

"Don't hide your true self
for the sake of fitting in.
Be okay with standing out."

TAEHYUNG INSPIRATIONS QUOTES

"Being yourself is
a revolutionary act that inspires
others to do the same."

"You are unique
and irreplaceable. Embrace your
individuality and let it be your strength."

TAEHYUNG INSPIRATIONS QUOTES

"Being okay
with being yourself is the ultimate
act of self-love and self-empowerment.

"Don't let society's expectations define who you should be. Embrace your own path and be proud of it."

TAEHYUNG INSPIRATIONS QUOTES

"The world is enriched by
your authentic presence. Embrace it
and make your mark."

"Being okay
with being yourself is a journey of self-discovery and self-acceptance."

"You are a work of art,
 and every brushstroke that makes you
who you are is beautiful."

"Don't compare yourself to others.
Embrace your uniqueness
and let it shine brightly."

TAEHYUNG INSPIRATIONS QUOTES

"Being true to yourself is the key
 to finding your purpose and
living a fulfilling life."

"You have a voice that is
meant to be heard.
Be okay with
expressing your true self."

TAEHYUNG INSPIRATIONS QUOTES

"Your individuality
is a gift to the world. Embrace it
and share it with confidence."

TAEHYUNG INSPIRATIONS QUOTES

"Being yourself is a constant reminder that you are enough, just as you are."

TAEHYUNG INSPIRATIONS QUOTES

"Don't be afraid
to show your true colors. Embrace your
authenticity and let it paint your world."

TAEHYUNG INSPIRATIONS QUOTES

"Being okay with being yourself i
s a journey of
self-acceptance and self-love."

TAEHYUNG INSPIRATIONS QUOTES

"You are worthy
of love and acceptance, simply
for being who you are."

"Authenticity is magnetic.
Embrace your true self and attract the
right people into your life."

TAEHYUNG INSPIRATIONS QUOTES

"Being true to yourself is
a form of rebellion against societal norms.
Embrace it and redefine the rules."

"Don't dim your light to fit in.
Shine brightly and inspire others to do the
same."

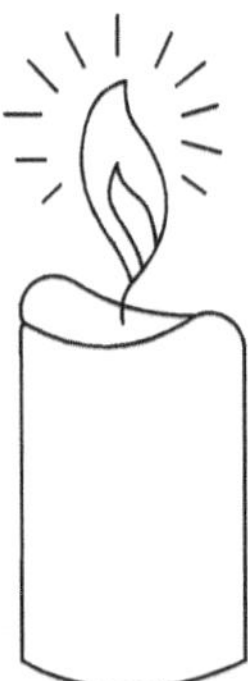

TAEHYUNG INSPIRATIONS QUOTES

"Your uniqueness is a
gift that sets you apart.
Be okay with being one-of-a-kind."

"Being yourself is a lifelong commitment to honoring your true essence."

TAEHYUNG INSPIRATIONS QUOTES

"You are a
masterpiece in progress.
Embrace your journey and
trust in your own growth."

"Don't seek
validation from others.
Be okay with validating yourself
and owning your worth."

"Being okay
with being yourself is
a radical act of self-empowerment
and self-expression."

"Your true self is
a beacon of light. Embrace it
and let it guide you on your path."

TAEHYUNG INSPIRATIONS QUOTES

"You were born to be yourself,
not a replica of someone else.
Embrace your authenticity."

"Being true to yourself is an
act of courage
that inspires others to do the same."

TAEHYUNG INSPIRATIONS QUOTES

"You don't need to conform
to society's standards.
Be okay with being your own unique self."

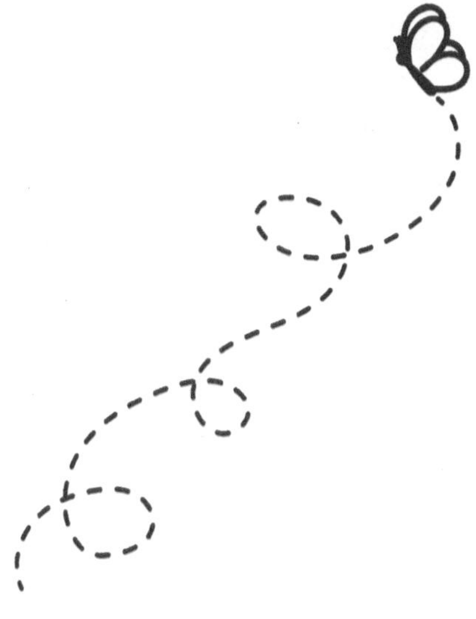

TAEHYUNG INSPIRATIONS QUOTES

"Embrace your quirks
and idiosyncrasies. They are
 what make you beautifully human."

TAEHYUNG INSPIRATIONS QUOTES

"Being okay
with being yourself is a
revolutionary act of self-acceptance
and self-love."

"Your true self is
your greatest asset. Embrace it
and let it guide you to greatness."

"Don't be afraid
to show your true colors.
Embrace your authenticity
and let it paint your world."

"Being true to yourself is a
 form of freedom
that liberates your spirit."

"You are an original masterpiece.
Embrace your own canvas
and create your unique story."

"Being okay
with being yourself is
the greatest gift you can give
to yourself and the world."

TAEHYUNG INSPIRATIONS QUOTES

"Your true self is a magnet for love and positive energy. Embrace it and let it attract what you deserve."

TAEHYUNG INSPIRATIONS QUOTES

"Don't apologize
for being yourself. Embrace it
and celebrate your own authenticity."

TAEHYUNG INSPIRATIONS QUOTES

"Being true to yourself is
a lifelong commitment to
honoring your own truth and values."

JUNGKOOK
INSPIRATIONS QUOTES

JUNGKOOK INSPIRATIONS QUOTES

"You are extraordinary,
 simply by being yourself.
Embrace your own greatness
and let it shine."

JUNGKOOK INSPIRATIONS QUOTES

"Excellence is achieved
when you commit to always
doing your best."

JUNGKOOK INSPIRATIONS QUOTES

"Your best effort is a reflection
of your character and dedication."

JUNGKOOK INSPIRATIONS QUOTES

"In every endeavor,
strive to leave no room for
regret by giving it your all."

JUNGKOOK INSPIRATIONS QUOTES

"Success comes to those who
consistently push
themselves to do their best."

"The satisfaction of knowing
you gave it your best is
a reward in itself."

JUNGKOOK INSPIRATIONS QUOTES

"Consistently giving
your best effort is the key
to personal growth and fulfillment."

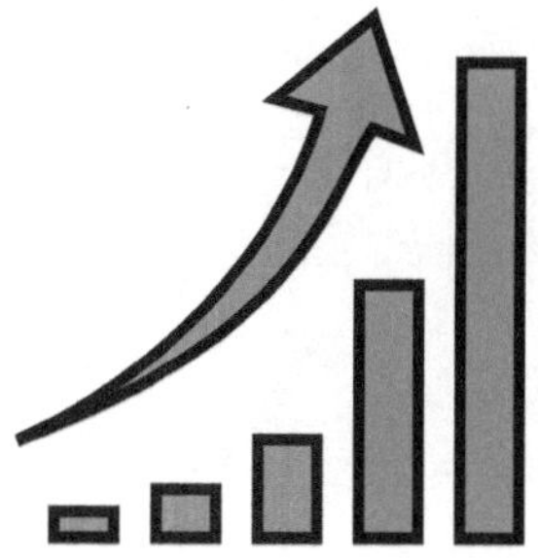

JUNGKOOK INSPIRATIONS QUOTES

You owe it
 to yourself to always strive
for greatness by doing your best."

JUNGKOOK INSPIRATIONS QUOTES

"Don't settle
for mediocrity when
you have the ability to
always do your best."

JUNGKOOK INSPIRATIONS QUOTES

"Your best effort paves the
way for extraordinary achievements and
limitless possibilities."

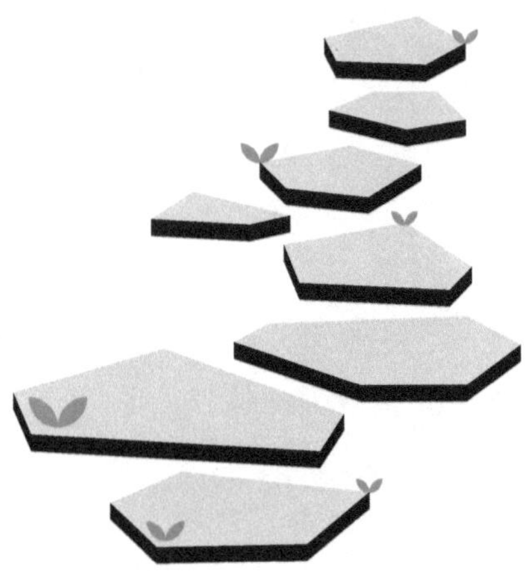

JUNGKOOK INSPIRATIONS QUOTES

"Be proud of the work
 you do by always
giving it your best shot."

"Every day is
an opportunity to show up
and give it your absolute best."

JUNGKOOK INSPIRATIONS QUOTES

"Your best effort today
sets the foundation for a brighter
and more successful tomorrow."

"In the pursuit of greatness,
always strive to give your best
in everything you do."

JUNGKOOK INSPIRATIONS QUOTES

"The path to success is
 paved with the consistent effort
of always doing your best."

JUNGKOOK INSPIRATIONS QUOTES

"You have
the power to make
a difference by always bringing
your best to the table."

JUNGKOOK INSPIRATIONS QUOTES

"Your best effort is
a reflection of your self-worth
and belief in your capabilities."

JUNGKOOK INSPIRATIONS QUOTES

"Never underestimate
the impact of always doing your best;
it can change your life."

JUNGKOOK INSPIRATIONS QUOTES

"Greatness is not
achieved overnight; it is the
result of always giving your best."

JUNGKOOK INSPIRATIONS QUOTES

"Your best effort
sets the standard for the
quality of work you produce."

"When you consistently
give your best, success becomes
an inevitable outcome."

"Your best effort is
the foundation upon which you
build your dreams."

JUNGKOOK INSPIRATIONS QUOTES

"Strive for excellence
by always giving your best,
even when no one is watching."

"Success is not guaranteed,
but your best effort ensures you
have no regrets."

JUNGKOOK INSPIRATIONS QUOTES

"By doing your best,
you inspire others to do the same
and create a ripple effect of greatness."

"Consistently giving your best is
a testament to your commitment
to personal growth and improvement."

JUNGKOOK INSPIRATIONS QUOTES

"Your best effort is
a reflection of your character
and work ethic."

JUNGKOOK INSPIRATIONS QUOTES

"Do your best
not only for the end result but
also for the satisfaction of knowing
you gave it your all."

JUNGKOOK INSPIRATIONS QUOTES

"Every step forward begins
with giving your best effort in
the present moment."

"By always doing your best,
you open doors to opportunities
you never thought possible."

JUNGKOOK INSPIRATIONS QUOTES

"Strive to make each day
count by always giving your best
in everything you do."

"Your best effort
may not always lead to success,
but it guarantees personal growth
and resilience."

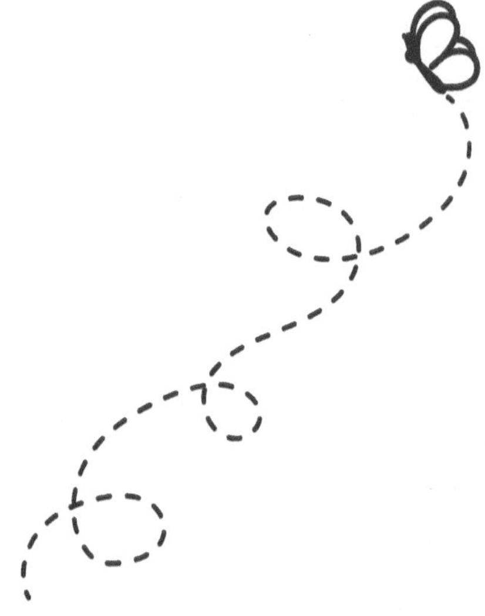

JUNGKOOK INSPIRATIONS QUOTES

"Give your best even when
the odds are stacked against you; you
never know what miracles can happen."

Your best effort
fuels the fire within you
to achieve extraordinary results."

JUNGKOOK INSPIRATIONS QUOTES

"When you consistently do your best,
you become a force to be reckoned with."

"Make it a habit to give
your best in every endeavor,
and success will follow.

JUNGKOOK INSPIRATIONS QUOTES

"The mark of a true champion is
their unwavering commitment
to always do their best."

"Your best effort is
a reflection of your dedication
to self-improvement and growth."

JUNGKOOK INSPIRATIONS QUOTES

"By always doing your best,
you defy limitations and
surpass your own expectations."

"In every challenge,
remember to bring your best self
and watch the magic unfold."

JUNGKOOK INSPIRATIONS QUOTES

"Your best effort is
a testament to your commitment
to personal excellence."

"Don't settle for anything
less than your best;
the world deserves to see your
greatness."

JUNGKOOK INSPIRATIONS QUOTES

"Your best effort is
the stepping stone to a life filled
with fulfillment and achievement."

"Success is not a destination; it's a journey of consistently doing your best."

"By always giving your best,
 you create a positive impact on
yourself and those around you."

"Your best effort
sets the stage for success
and opens doors to new possibilities."

JUNGKOOK INSPIRATIONS QUOTES

"Don't be satisfied
with average; challenge yourself
to always give your best."

JUNGKOOK INSPIRATIONS QUOTES

"Your best effort
may require sacrifice
and hard work, but
it will always be worth it."

JUNGKOOK INSPIRATIONS QUOTES

"In every endeavor,
remember to bring your A-game
and give it your absolute best."

JUNGKOOK INSPIRATIONS QUOTES

"By always doing your best,
you become a role model for others
and inspire them to reach
their full potential."

BTS
INSPIRATIONS QUOTES

BTS INSPIRATIONS QUOTES

"Dream, hope, and keep going.
BTS taught us that even the smallest steps can lead to great success."

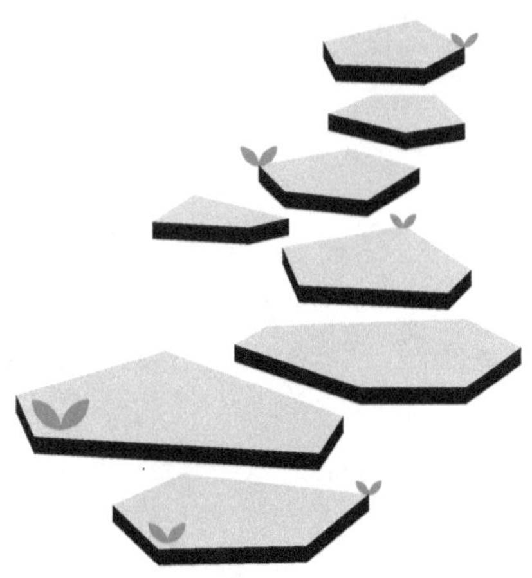

BTS INSPIRATIONS QUOTES

"In a world where you can
be anything, be like BTS – spreading love,
positivity, and inspiring change."

BTS INSPIRATIONS QUOTES

"BTS reminds us that our true strength lies in our ability to lift each other up and stand together."

BTS INSPIRATIONS QUOTES

"Through their music,
BTS has shown us the power of
vulnerability and the healing it brings."

"BTS teaches us that success is
not just about achieving our dreams but
also staying true to ourselves along the
way."

BTS INSPIRATIONS QUOTES

"In a world filled with noise,
BTS's music acts as a soothing melody
that resonates with our souls."

BTS INSPIRATIONS QUOTES

"BTS inspires us to embrace our flaws,
celebrate our uniqueness,
 and love ourselves unconditionally."

BTS INSPIRATIONS QUOTES

"Through their lyrics,
BTS encourages us to find our own voice
and speak our truths with courage."

"BTS's journey from underdogs
to global icons is a testament to the power
of passion, perseverance, and hard
work."

BTS INSPIRATIONS QUOTES

"BTS's messages of self-acceptance and unity remind us that we are all worthy of love and belonging."

BTS INSPIRATIONS QUOTES

"BTS encourages us
to dream big, work hard,
and never give up on our aspirations, no
matter how challenging they may seem."

BTS INSPIRATIONS QUOTES

"BTS's music transcends language
barriers and touches hearts
around the world, reminding us of our
shared humanity."

"BTS's success is a testament to
the power of teamwork, mutual
respect, and supporting
one another's growth."

BTS INSPIRATIONS QUOTES

"BTS teaches us that
true strength comes from
acknowledging our weaknesses
and striving to become better
versions of ourselves."

BTS INSPIRATIONS QUOTES

"Through their philanthropy
and acts of kindness, BTS shows us the
importance of giving back and making a
positive impact in the world."

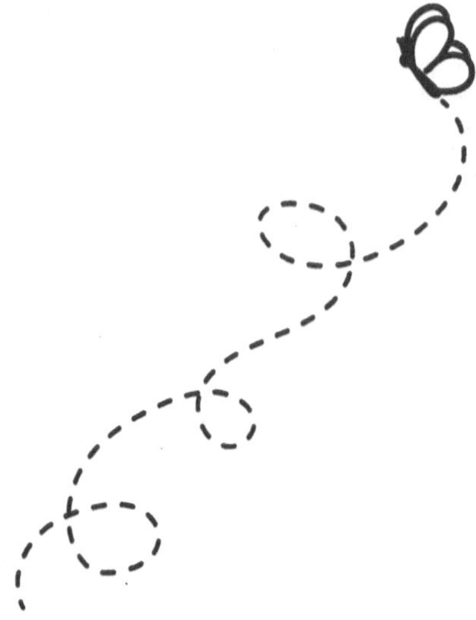

"BTS's authenticity and genuine connection with their fans remind us of the power of genuine human connections."

BTS INSPIRATIONS QUOTES

"BTS's lyrics are a source of comfort, providing solace during difficult times and reminding us that we are never alone in our struggles."

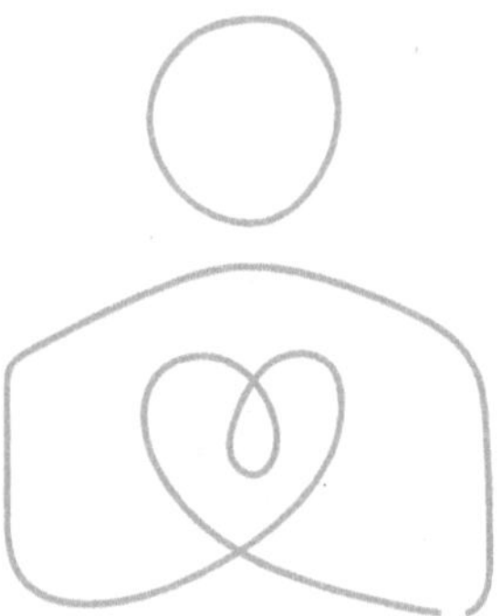

BTS INSPIRATIONS QUOTES

"BTS's humility
and gratitude serve as
a reminder to remain grounded
and appreciate every step
of our own journey."

"BTS's positive influence
on mental health awareness
encourages us to prioritize self-care
and seek help when needed."

"BTS's lyrics empower us
to challenge societal norms,
break free from limitations, and
create our own path in life."

CONCLUSION

As you close the final chapter of this book, may the inspiring words of BTS continue to resonate in your heart. Let their profound wisdom and uplifting messages guide you on your journey toward hope, love and self-discovery.
Just as BTS has touched countless lives with its music and quotes, let this collection of inspirational quotes remind you that dreams are worth pursuing, and that with perseverance, we can overcome any obstacle.
As we bid farewell, remember that the power to make a difference lies within each of us, and that together we can create a brighter, kinder world. Keep the passion alive and make these words a source of strength and inspiration. "Love yourself, talk about yourself" and embrace the magic that awaits you. Thank you for joining us on this journey of inspiration and discovery with BTS.

www.ingramcontent.com/pod-product-compliance
Lightning Source LLC
LaVergne TN
LVHW090554140726
843272LV00039B/342